Mercury

ALSO BY PHILLIS LEVIN

Temples and Fields
The Afterimage

PHILLIS LEVIN

Mercury

PENGUIN POETS

PENGUIN BOOKS
Published by the Penguin Group
Penguin Putnam Inc., 375 Hudson Street,
New York, New York 10014, U.S.A.
Penguin Books Ltd, 27 Wrights Lane, London W8 5TZ, England
Penguin Books Australia Ltd, Ringwood, Victoria, Australia
Penguin Books Canada Ltd, 10 Alcorn Avenue,
Toronto, Ontario, Canada M4V 3B2
Penguin Books (N.Z.) Ltd, 182–190 Wairau Road,
Auckland 10, New Zealand

Penguin Books Ltd, Registered Offices:
Harmondsworth, Middlesex, England

First published in Penguin Books 2001

1 3 5 7 9 10 8 6 4 2

LIBRARY OF CONGRESS CATALOGING-IN-PUBLICATION DATA
Levin, Phillis, 1954–
Mercury / Phillis Levin.
p. cm. — (Penguin poets)
ISBN 0-14-058928-7
I. Title.

PS3562.E88966 M47 2001
811'.54—dc21   00-062409

Printed in the United States of America
Set in Granjon
Designed by Suvi Asch

Acknowledgments

Grateful acknowledgment is made to the editors of the following publications, in which these poems first appeared:

American Literary Review: "In a Haystack," "Elegy for a Magnolia"

Barrow Street: "Afternoon Sketch," "Company," "Final Request," "Conversation in an Empty Room," "Confession of an Alchemist"

The Kenyon Review: "Archaic Notions," "Meditation on A and The"

The Nation: "The Blizzard," "Unsolicited Survey"

The New Criterion: "Cumulus," "Double Figure," "Georgic," "Ontological"

The New Republic: "A Portrait"

The New Yorker: "Part," "Soon," "Face to Face"

The Paris Review: "The Lector"

Ploughshares: "Mercury"

Poetry International: "Table Manners"

TriQuarterly: "Futile Exercise," "Intervals in Early August," "There," "Morning Exercise," "On the Other Hand"

Verse: "Fugue"

Washington Square: "Nocturne," "Nativity with Mother, Child, and Chair," "Dancing with Allen Ginsberg"

"Ontological" appeared in *The Best American Poetry 1998,* edited by John Hollander, Series Editor David Lehman (New York: Scribner, 1998); "Cumulus," "A Portrait," and "Part" appeared in *The New Bread Loaf Anthology of Contemporary American Poetry,* edited by Michael Collier and Stanley Plumly (University Press of New England, 1999); "Face to Face" appeared in *How Poetry Works* by Phil Roberts (Penguin UK, 2000).

The author would like to express her gratitude to The MacDowell Colony and to Yaddo, havens that made many of the poems in this book possible; to the Graduate Research Board of the University of Maryland, College Park, for a Creative and Performing Arts Grant that supported the completion of this collection; and to the Trustees of the Amy Lowell Poetry Travelling Scholarship, for the gift of time to write and revise while living in Rome.

For their generous encouragement and criticism, special thanks are due to David Baker, Bruce Bond, Peter Covino, Sharon Dolin, Johanna Keller, Charles Martin, James McCorkle, Molly Peacock, Marjetica Potrč, Elfie Raymond, James Reiss, Mark Rudman, Grace Schulman, and Tomaž Šalamun. Rosanna Warren's insight has been crucial.

My profound thanks, requiring a move into the first person, are due to my friend and fellow poet Elizabeth Macklin, whose pencil has touched so many of these lines. I would also like to thank my editor, Caroline J. White, for her essential support, and the two guardian angels of this collection, Dawn Drzal and Peter Mandelstam.

Contents

PART ONE

Part   3
Ontological   4
Cumulus   6
Morning Exercise   7
Nocturne   8
Final Request   9
Face to Face   10
Conversation in an Empty Room   11
Instead of a Letter   12
Afternoon Sketch   15
A Portrait   16
Fugue   17
Mercury   20

PART TWO

Archaic Notions   27
There   30
Nativity with Mother, Child, and Chair   31
Table Manners   33
Elegy for a Magnolia   35
Dancing with Allen Ginsberg   39
Double Figure   41
Beginning to Count   42

PART THREE

Unsolicited Survey   53

Intervals in Early August   55

On the Other Hand   59

Soon   60

The Blizzard   61

Company   62

Futile Exercise   63

Georgic   66

In a Haystack   67

The Lector   69

Confession of an Alchemist   71

Meditation on A and The   73

III. The metal, etc. 2. Old Chem. *a. One of the five elementary "principles" of which all material substances were supposed to be compounded; also called* spirit *1471.*

—Oxford Universal Dictionary

. . . and the elements when moved were separated and carried continually, some one way, some another. As, when grain is shaken and winnowed by fans and other instruments used in the threshing of corn, the close and heavy particles are borne away and settle in one direction, and the loose and light particles in another. In this manner, the four kinds or elements were then shaken by the receiving vessel, which, moving like a winnowing machine, scattered far away from one another the elements most unlike, and forced the most similar elements into close contact.

—PLATO, Timaeus

PART ONE

Part

Of something, separate, not
Whole; a role, something to play
While one is separate or parting;

Also a piece, a section, as in
Part of me is here, part of me
Is missing; an essential portion,

Something falling to someone
In division; a particular voice
Or instrument (also the score

For it), or line of music;
The line where the hair
Is parted. A verb: to break

Or suffer the breaking of,
Become detached,
Broken; to go from, leave,

Take from, sever, as in
Lord, part me from him,
I cannot bear to ever

Ontological

for Elfie Raymond

If it were not so bright,
Not so dark;
If there had been another hour,

Another storm,
Something to keep track of
Or something to hold at bay;

If there had been no bird
On the barest tree,
With one bitter crumb in its mouth,

One little speck;
If the honey surrounding that crumb
Had not been sweet,

If the evening had been less silent,
Humming one note
Without leaving any name,

Calling me to a field whose sickle moon
Made it clear
That nothing would speak;

If the way to the field
Had been less glorious,
A drop of dew beside a milkweed seed,

A ladybug scampering toward light,
And flowers on fire
Swaying among tall grasses—

A river of paper lanterns at dawn;
If the gift had not been
A cluster of wild cyclamen,

Whose scent continued
To spill its horn of plenty,
Outlasting the final kiss of day.

Cumulus

They, too, labor,
And if we envy them we should remember
How brief their stay in the ether is.

Unfolding without reason, like forgiveness,
Or summoning
Themselves at the wind's bidding, they flee.

We do not know where they go, we go
As carelessly, as helplessly, finally
Too full of time.

But we are true
To ourselves so rarely, while they are always
Open to darkness, squandering light.

A floating prison, a dream-balloon,
The setting sun's
Chameleon, or the sliding screen of the moon—

When nothing else contains us we turn to them,
And all we ever gather appears
Less tangible.

Morning Exercise

Line by line I unremember you:
Places your mouth hid, and where
Your teeth almost bit through
My skin, leaving a necklace

Whose blue pearls lingered
For days—a few scattered across
My chest, as if you broke a strand
Whenever you left. Say nothing

About how you are, or who
You have been, say nothing
Now that there is nothing to say.

It is useless to ask for a word,
Useless to know what is true.
Line by line I unremember you.

Nocturne

Two waterfalls we were
The night we lived all night

Together like two drops
Of rain slipping

From god's gold back
After a day in the garden

Before the world began:
We were a single stream

And then arose
Pouring through each other

No more than silk and fur
Entering and entered

Until a cooling drop
Of light was all we were.

Final Request

If I die I will need a cross
To carry me to the next world,
The one I do not believe in.
But a cross will carry me
Anyway. When I meet the dory
That overturns despair—
When he who could not
Let love carry him over

Weeps, finally weeps there,
Where he does not believe
He will go—my arms will be
So cruel. Whether or not
They hold him, whether or not
I want to they will want to.

Face to Face

I sing of love, sacred and profane,
Of knowledge lost, strangely found again;
And time that travels with us till we die,
Boarding the train, waving a last goodbye.

What I have learned appears on every leaf,
For the first sign of growth is belief;
The countersign of life is a lie,
Following fast after No and Why.

I have believed in truth, beholding it,
And many times have been deceived by it;
For love is double, even when it joins,
And dispossesses everything it owns.

Conversation in an Empty Room

You were still alive, then.

Yes, I was.

And we had a lot to say to each other.

But not enough.

There was a high level of chatter, very intelligent.

Of course, us being who we were.

But I was always at the edge of disappointing
Or annoying you, or delighting you,
Which was worse,
Since I feared you might want me,
And I did not want to be wanted.
I wanted to be heard, to listen, standing
In a room with you—

Really, you could have lain down beside me
At least once. It wouldn't have been
The end of the world.

But it would have been.

And now that it is?

Instead of a Letter

I.

Regarding the weather, whatever it does
It is certainly here, asking us
To leave ourselves behind, to listen
A while to the solemn procession
Of rain on a roof, sliding into gutters,
Distilling itself in a country
Relatively free of gargoyles.

II.

The word on the tip of my tongue is gone.
So is the one that moments ago
Lodged itself under my lids, also the one
That early this morning was brighter
Than anything else on the list for the day.

III.

What are you referring to exactly,
My good soldier, lush stoic, itinerant friend,
Whose letters cannot arrive
Because they answer the one I never could send?

IV.

Relatively free, did you say, and what
Do you mean by that—or will you avoid my eyes,
As usual, filling the room with innuendoes?
Was it you or I who said that
Way back when, with no time to go
And all the time in the world?
If it is I, what did I mean, and if it is you,
What perfect contradiction will prevail?

V.

If it was presumptuous of me to suggest
That we live in god's pocket,
To pronounce in the middle of our goodbye
Something that salted the flesh
Of your nouns, as if I could not accept
The lack of irony in your voice
When you informed me of your ardor,
There being nothing more dangerous than passionate
Self-deception, then forgive me now for trespassing
On your sleep, which has lasted longer
Than the type endured by princesses.

VI.

You have no idea how much I held back.
Then again, I have no idea how much you did either.

VII.

Your attempt to make things easy as pie for an hour
Only made things difficult thereafter.
I accept complexity, being simple in my pleasures,
And am capable of forgetting almost anything
That gets in the way of joy, for as long as it lasts.
But those projections into the near and distant future
About happiness and all the rest, etc.,
Were really over the top, considering.

VIII.

One breeze in particular was accompanied
By a small flock of gulls who were
So sparsely dispersed across the sky's arena
That the stars seemed more indelible
Than usual, and all of this occurred
As a figure out of nowhere crossed a square
In the neighborhood of one tree in particular.

IX.

Touch me, the letters say,
Knowing the ink is dry,
That nothing will ever change them
Unless it does so utterly.

Afternoon Sketch

There is nothing she wants to do,
Nothing she wants to say.
But a late summer bud
Catches her eye, and the clank
Of an iron gate quickens her heart.

She will sit here for now and feel
Very little, she will look
Many years at the same
Shade of sorrow.
It is enough, more than enough.

A Portrait

It was getting dark, and all the while
Something in you was coming forward,
The way a mountain appears to loom
At the end of day. We were talking

About myriad things as dusk dissolved
The table between us, where a bottle
Of wine floated in summer's aura.
Then the light changed, your profile

Sharpened, and suddenly I saw
A side of you that could kill.
Calmly I sat, watching something
That all along had been hiding

In the background, under your shyness,
Under your stillness. Your shoulders,
Broad enough to hold years of silence,
Bore no weapon, but surely your hands

Had carried one, reluctantly, securely.
And your arms folded before me
Posed an enormous question
Forbidding any answer.

Fugue

since I am here
and you are there and you

are there and I am here
it is impossible he said

she said after a while
without a word

so they agreed
after a while

happily sadly
falling away

from each other
without turning

seeing it all
before them

fall behind them
before turning

under a sky
whose constellations

didn't even glimmer
no it wasn't late enough

for that to happen
now or then

though now
and then they see it

all before them
hear each other feel

each other breathing
near each other

far enough away
for it to burn

like one of those events
in the heavens

that happened long ago
so far away

it can finally
be seen

though clearly
no one saw it

taking place
as it befell

least of all themselves
who weren't here

when they were there
to say what was

between them
in a landscape

where nothing
occurred as far

as one can tell
that is recorded

anywhere
by anyone

least of all
themselves

who had
been there

Mercury

A vial of it: dusty, warm
From being held so long
In my hand; the little cork that fit

So well, the cap I would undo
In secret, sprawling on the floor
Of the basement, recalling a scene

From Kafka, or glancing in horror
At the old vermilion volume
On Chinese torture, or savoring

The sage-green suede
Of the Rubaiyat, before I ever
Got to Freud. The same dust

Gilded the Harvard Classics,
Uniform in their jackets,
Their leather dry and glossy,

While the glass vial beckoned
With its mysterious fluid
That could bifurcate and scatter,

Rolling, pausing, pooling,
Some dots escaping
Into cracks in the linoleum,

But most of them retrieved,
Succumbing to each other
As I gathered them together

With the slightest pressure,
The liquid growing dimmer
Each time it was restored,

Its ratio of loss too minor,
Too gradual, for Father
To suspect what I had done.

Why was it there, hiding
On his desk behind a pipe
With the face of Mephistopheles?

What experiment forgotten,
Abandoned, untried, what badge
Of glory or failure did it signify,

That small, heavy vial
Whose promise was a murky
Wave of buoyancy, an innocence

Of having, of breaking—
Creating without consequence
Droplets forsaking

The sea whence they came
Without a seam, or cry of protest,
Or any sound of severance

At the source, the minuscule
Remainder a reminder of the refusal
To be destroyed, the singularity

Of every silver bead that briefly
Lived apart from the whole
Before merging and returning

To the vessel I would hold
And shake and spill, and finally
Refill, in a ritual of parting,

Pouring being into
Being, pondering its nature
In the open field of my hand,

My limited supply of a substance
Infinite in its divisibility
And equally indivisible,

An unborn mass of matter
Immortal and mute as the sleeping
Figure eight (not a number,

Really, but the god of numbers)
That Father drew on paper,
Never closed so never ending,

Though once he said to me
In the morning, just as the light
Began to swim through my shade,

Do you think I will always be here?—
As if he were unlocking a door
Between us; and what could I say,

Either way it was unspeakable,
And how could he know
His question altered everything,

That the earth began to change
As the thought of his being no more
Took root, dividing him

From me, from the sky I appealed to,
Unanswered: O god of alchemy
And currency, patron of traders,

Travellers, and thieves, inventor
Of the lyre, master of dreams,
Leader of the Graces, bearer

Of the message that tears
Odysseus from Circe, Aeneas
From Dido, guardian of the departed,

Do not quicken my heart with hope
Anymore, but if you do remember
That I, like the metal you give

Your name to, rejoin if pulled asunder.

PART TWO

Archaic Notions

*Time, then, and the heavens came into being at the same
instant in order that, having been created together, if ever there
was to be a dissolution of them, they might be dissolved
together.*

—*Plato*, Timaeus

I used to open drawers by focusing my attention on the knobs,
But I stopped doing this because it made people nervous.
Actually, I never looked long enough to open anything
Or move a piece of furniture an inch, but because I believed

It was possible, I could live in the world. My greatest fear
Was of being discovered—though I never imagined the details
Of the aftermath, my irrevocable exile, due less to impatience
With fantasy than a general tendency to forget trouble easily.

Belief in my power persisted, untested, after my conversion
To the scientific method; and the magnetic pole of abstraction
Only served to complicate the problem, distancing me further
From common sense: for example, if the properties of a feather

Allowed it to float in such a leisurely manner, then ten feathers
Should be ten times lighter, and so on, for wouldn't the quality
Of lightness multiply, increasing tenfold? Therefore, I could fill
A sack with feathers, walk to the edge of a cliff and jump,

Holding a bag that would carry me, very slowly, to the bottom
Of a valley. Of course this contraption wasn't necessary,
Since I was able to fly. But it seemed to be an experiment
Worth trying, given the right conditions. Soon I'd settle down,

More preoccupied by a current of electricity or the private life
Of trees, how a nugget of coal transmogrified or a waterdrop
Became a cloud, than with a question my father couldn't answer,
A question that wouldn't go away, born the night he told me

How the universe began. There was nothing (. . .), then there was
Something. It wasn't hard to understand. *But what was before
The nothing?* My head hurt whenever I thought about it—a pulse
Of darkness and light, specks of dust expanding, contracting,

An accidental spore pollinating galaxies—a physical pain
That started in my mind, as if the creation were happening
There, spreading into a sensation whose rhythm is familiar
To all curious children. Thinking about a time before time,

Trying to find a place for it seconds before it moved across
The border of eternity, swept into the cold arms of a clock
Feeding it to a corps of ravenous numbers, wasn't a good idea,
Even as a metaphor, for seeing, with eyes closed, a glimpse

Of the beginning was as dangerous as looking at the sun.
But matter should have made more sense, and whatever
Nothing was before it came to be the thing it came to be
Should have cooperated, finally, considering the time

And energy spent on solving the problem. *Where was I
When you were a little girl,* I reportedly asked my mother,
Forming a conundrum whose elliptical nature owed as much
To confusion and caution as to any metaphysical disposition.

All children are philosophers. They really have no choice
In the matter, for they do not know the frame of reference
Into which they were born, and so the genuine insight of a query
Turning our preconceptions topsy-turvy originates in a particular

Mixture of ignorance, audacity, and wonder: something
That requires years of skepticism and humility to replicate
Adequately. Notice how sex and the basic forces of attraction
Needn't enter the equation, if the issue is raised in this fashion.

The explanation was impersonal, cellular, and that may disturb
Both parent and child, since a being wants to take some credit
For being. Assuming there was an I before I was born is not far
From assuming that there was something before the nothing.

But I had a long way to go. And it occurs to me now that more
Terrible than not existing and never having existed is conceiving
Of a universe that did not exist. Calling one to mind, so to speak.
Then there wouldn't even be a place for nonbeing to call home.

There

for Steffen Stelzer

It was somewhere else,
Not in my heart.
The room not moving
But on the moving one,

A shape ablaze
With color and scent.
Not here, but there:
Not with me or for me,

Not mother, father, light.
But light made it happen.
Dark pushed it away

And made it closer, too.
It was cool, separate,
Just beginning to be.

Nativity with Mother, Child, and Chair

Why did the back of a chair
Make me stare at my mother?
What about that wooden latticework
Made me see what she said

Was a lie—as if seeing through it
I could see through her.
She was trying very hard
To cover it up, not because

She didn't want to lie,
But because she saw I knew
Something I wasn't supposed to.
"It isn't true," I said

To an abstract flower,
Curlicues and slats of emptiness
Through which I clearly saw her
Looking at me in fear.

"You lied," I said, using a word
I didn't know I knew.
"It's a *white* lie," she said.
That was something new.

I'd never heard a color
Used that way before: white
Must be the worst kind of lie,
The one a mother would tell.

The chair between us
Cast its shadow.
I crouched like a harmless animal,
Watching her mouth move.

But why was I behind a chair,
Holding her between its bars,
In plain sight, where anyone
Could see that I was hiding

From her and she was hiding
That she was hiding from me.

Table Manners

What do you need?

> A knife, a fork, a spoon.

Is the order important?

> For my purposes, yes.

Say more about this, please.

> The knife, first. A knife does more
> than the rest.

Do you mean when it comes to eating?

> Yes. It can cut, it can spear,
> it can smear honey, as well as do damage.

Why a fork, then?

> It is the most beautiful of the three:
> the curve of its tines, especially,
> and the way it rests in the hand.

And the spoon, what about the spoon?

> Not so important, unless one is a child—
> though for soup there is really no choice,
> unless one resorts to nothing at all.

Don't you need it for anything else?

> Melons, maybe. And the mirror
> a spoon can be, or the image of love in repose.

But it isn't necessary.

> I can do without it, I can do without
> almost anything, if necessary.

Elegy for a Magnolia

Sometimes I dream of her again, in the backyard
Of our brick, stone, and clapboard house in Paterson,
Where the last I heard a black minister was living

With his family. I ring the bell and he or his wife
Answers, but they don't invite me in. Sometimes
I implore them, and even though I am no one

To them they let me in. First I want to see
If they have changed my bedroom wallpaper,
Whose crisscrossing leaves made a net

Keeping me from the kingdom hidden behind
My wall. Is the crystal chandelier still there,
Dangling above the dining room table,

The shadow-caster, the rainbow-maker
My mother and grandmother monthly took apart,
Removing each long, elaborate strand of tears,

Carefully setting the machinery of beauty
Onto a cotton cloth, unhooking each drop
From its delicate wire hook, lining them up

From small to large and wiping them clean,
Then reattaching them before assembling
All the strands on their glass skeleton—

Re-hooking the biggest crystal last,
The one that hung alone, in the center,
Like a cold colossal raindrop refusing to fall.

But most of all I want to see the magnolia,
The great old tree standing at the end
Of the yard, its thick lacquer leaves

Obscuring another neighbor's property,
Its huge magenta seedpods frightening me
(As if an unnameable creature were trapped

Inside, ready to hatch at any hour), utterly
Alien-looking, compared to everything else
Surrounding our house. Hydrangeas blue

As dusk, red tulips and apricot roses,
A bed of daffodils, a slender lilac bush
And a row of rhododendrons and azaleas,

Even the subtle well of the purple petunia,
A birch with the legs of a zebra upside-down,
And the sudden buttery-yellow forsythia

Cascading midwinter could not prepare me
For that extravagant surprise, a blossoming
Too quickly turning prodigal and sweet.

Perhaps the only proof that my mother's mother
Loved anything in the world beside her children
And their children (and her husband, Philip Engel,

Who died the year before my parents married,
My mother pinning a tiny black ribbon
To the petticoat of her white wedding gown),

The only living sign my grandmother gave
Of her grief, occurred the day my little brother,
In anger, struck the magnolia, hitting it

With a stick and cutting it so deeply
Its sap ran and glistened in the sun—a wound
She could see from the window overlooking

The yard, where she would sit and watch us
As we played: *The tree is bleeding, the tree
Is bleeding,* she cried. *For shame, for shame,*

It's alive. As she shrieked at him in a voice
I had never heard, something kin to lightning
Ran through me, as if her cry

Were the sap of the stricken tree, its stream
The fine, searing flame of her desire
To seal the memory of what she had lost:

Her mother and her father, her good husband,
Then her brothers and sisters, all of them
Dying of natural causes at home in America.

For though she once referred to postcards
From distant relatives who wrote infrequently,
Then not at all, who were "transported" finally,

No one could tell how much she ever thought
Of those who said they had no reason to go,
Or no way if they had reason, or of the country

A girl of twelve at the turn of the century
Left with her parents for good (*They can keep
Poland*), as she sat in triumph in her chair,

Watching my brother playing on her property,
A plot of land she and my grandfather bought
In 1940 in Paterson, New Jersey, moving

Closer to the river running beside the silk mills,
One owned by her husband, one by her father,
Where she built a proper, unassuming house

Whose border was marked by a tree sacred,
I later learned, to the Polish: the proud
Magnolia Lena Engel loved,

Whose lavish shade we lived in until she heard
Her neighbor of thirty years was moving away,
And the new one would be a different color.

Because of this my grandmother sold her house,
Waiting for a buyer who was white (she'd peek
Between the blinds whenever the bell rang,

Making believe no one was home if she saw
Someone dark through the curtain at the door),
And we moved with her to a flat, rural town,

Returning rarely to visit relatives. Sometimes
We'd pass by in the car, my father pausing
Before driving on (my mother wouldn't look),

Once my brother and I went alone, telling
No one we had gone, walking up the hill
To 19th Avenue, noticing how much smaller

The house was, how immaculate the lawn
And flowers tended by the family living there.
We wondered who they were, I wondered if

They'd let us see the backyard garden again.
Still the wound is burning, for shame.

Dancing with Allen Ginsberg

First of all, I didn't. Why not? From the start
You'll need to know how Mrs. Materasso,
Who long ago had been our first-grade teacher,
Appeared in the middle of a birthday party

And proceeded to tell a group of seventh-graders
About the evils of marijuana and hallucinogens,
Finishing her lesson just before he stepped in.
No way that she could know his father, Louis,

Lived in the house next door, or that Allen
Would be visiting, in for a day from the city;
No way she could predict that when she ran
Out of Marlboros, he'd reach into a box

Nestled in his breast pocket, and offer her
A cigarette she had to refuse. "What if he put
Something in it," she said the moment he left,
As if in fact he were the living illustration

For her lecture. I'd always wrongly assumed
He was crashing that party, never suspecting
The parents of the birthday boy had formally
Invited him, until I mentioned it to him

In 1993, and he made a point of correcting me,
When we met by chance on a street in Łodz,
The town my mother's mother was from.
He had come to celebrate the Polish edition

Of his poems, and I would soon be reading
Beside him, surrounded by roses thrown
By beautiful men. He looked frailer then,
Not the man who walked up to me one day

In May in the late Sixties, when all the girls
And boys were beginning to dance together.
He approached me, his white cotton shirt
Practically transparent from his sweat,

The dark hair on his chest showing through.
"Would you like to dance?" I could barely
Say no, but I did. "You're a wallflower,"
He whispered, stepping away to do the Twist

With R.T., who was freckled and chubby,
But seemed thoroughly happy in her body.

Double Figure

In a vast arena
I met a double figure
Looking like my mother,
As tall as my young father,

Welcoming me.
There was something to say
So I asked politely:
Are you happy together,

When did you die?
But they were still alive,
And we tore at each other

Without reason or mercy,
Remorse a dangling spider
Going without dinner.

Beginning to Count

in memory of Lena Salzberg Engel

In Salzburg, a taste of your maiden name,
Where dogs are muzzled to protect the public
And houses on the riverbank are watercolor

Yellow, pink, and gray, I realized I knew
A bit of German when I stepped into a bus
And heard the driver telling someone the fare.

In a bakery earlier that day, after I had chosen
What I wanted—pointing politely to a golden
Pastry shimmering behind the glass display—

An elderly woman followed me to my table,
Offering a beautiful slice of strudel, although
She was a stranger and the piece I had bought

Was in my hand. I don't know why she thought
She had to feed me, or why she sat so close
When I refused, visibly disheartened by my no,

That melted to yes when she insisted with such
Kindness, as if she had known me long ago.
Perhaps I reminded her of someone or my youth

Grazed a memory, but what could I say
Except thank you, without any words for
Sorry, I've had enough, I couldn't possibly,

Though it looks so good, as delicious
As mine, which is flaky and light, and filled
With apricot jam, just a wisp of sugar on top.

So we sat together in silence, once in a while
Smiling at each other, though something
About her expression made me want to weep.

But the purchase itself had been easy,
Unlike my problem days before, in Vienna,
When I tried to get some mustard

For my knockwurst, switching
From English to French, failing completely,
Though it seemed the most obvious thing

To go with a sausage; yet even when I found
A pencil and paper, and drew the picture
Of a jar, the waiter shook his baffled head

Until, as usual, the miraculous happened
As soon as I gave up, and someone tuned in
To my dilemma arrived with what appeared

To be a tube of toothpaste, only it was
Exactly what I needed: *Senf,* he said, *Senf,*
Removing the cap, happy to help me out.

From then on I expected nothing
To make sense, but meandering all day
In the liberty of being without speaking,

Relishing the infant joy of seeing the world
Without words, I began to distinguish
Certain familiar sounds, cadences wound

Like a bright ribbon tangled in a braid,
Syllables that wafted from an alley or sizzled
To the surface and actually meant something,

I was sure, though I didn't know what,
Or why I was being touched by the shadow
Of understanding, until it came to me

It was the trace of your Yiddish, which I never
Could grasp, since you saved it for my mother,
Who answered only in English, the two of you

Conducting an epic conversation consisting
Of non sequiturs and oblique connotations,
Patches of silence momentarily lit

By a nod or a sigh, or an occasional
I wouldn't be a-bit-sa-prized,
That pungent *a-bit-sa*

A vocable that regularly puzzled me.
Daily you and your daughter recounted all
The things I shouldn't know, or ever repeat:

I learned my lesson well one afternoon,
Astonishing Mr. Schlossberger, my refugee
Piano teacher, bidding him goodbye

By mimicking your very words that morning,
A curiously emphatic phrase you clearly
Translated as *Go in good health* when I asked.

It sounded like a variant of *God bless you,*
But apparently it meant *Go to hell,*
For after you shut the door behind him

I had to promise not to say that to anyone.
You wouldn't explain, but the look on his face
Made it plain I hadn't said what I thought.

You spoke your slightly broken English
With a strong accent, proud to discard
The past, guarding the keys to your dominion:

Chests of monogrammed silver and linen,
Doilies and coupons and glittering crystal,
Coasters and cake knives and candelabra,

Row upon row of bone china from England,
France, Czechoslovakia, scissors for cutting
A cluster of grapes, bowls for globes

Of sour candy and dishes for everything
Odd or rare—caviar, sweetbreads, kumquats,
Jumbo olives. Yet still you maintained

Your own version of kosher: pork forbidden
On any condition, unless unrecognized (thus
Forgiven), milk never cooked with meat

(But permitted in a glass beside it),
Shellfish never served inside the house,
With the exception of lobster, whose tails

Your perfect son delivered twice a year,
My uncle's delectable, mildly subversive gift,
Broiled and eaten on special disposable plates.

You resorted to Yiddish to keep me in the dark,
But when I was a child you often held me
On your lap and sang a counting song

That taught me almost nothing about numbers,
Only that its melody was sad and sweet,
Too sad for numbers, and that you sang

As a way of loving me. It must have been
Like *One, two, buckle my shoe,* but I knew
That *buckle* and *shoe* weren't numbers, too:

Ein, svei, drei, fee-ya (melancholy pause),
Fei mi-lus tee-ya. . . . Probably it went to ten,
But I didn't comprehend more than *three,*

Which in English you called *tree,* stopping
At every third step as you led me, sideways,
Down the stairs, hoping to avoid vertigo.

So when I stood in line with a friend
And it came time to buy tickets for a movie
Or the trolley, I understood enough to say

How many, murmuring *ein* or *svei*
Very quickly, like an imposter, for what if
The numbers weren't the same or I carried

Your inflection—would they guess the source
Of my error, and then what would happen?
If I stayed with *one* or *two,* they might not

Detect I was foreign, but I was afraid
Of going higher, having always shied away
From pronouncing German, despite

My love of Rilke, whose Elegies a man
From Berlin brought to my bed and recited
(Now that you are dead I can mention him).

For I must have known I could betray myself
With a simple, half-remembered locution,
And that's probably one of the things

You were trying so hard to teach me.
It wasn't for me, that language of secrets,
Of horrible gossip and desperate humor,

Sudden cries of anger, mirth, or grief:
I didn't want its taste on my tongue
And I didn't want to bring you back again.

After all, who wants to be torn in two,
To feel the bitterness rising in one's throat,
Then the hammer behind the eyes as a tear

Wells, spilling over against one's will until
The mouth cannot contain the salt of sorrow;
Who wants to hear a chicken being slaughtered,

Whether the means are holy or unholy,
And why must a prayer be uttered for anything
When the air is fed by the buzz of sacred bees?

I did not want to remember how you held me
As you sang, before you turned stony
And severe, frightening me and my brother,

Creeping up behind us if we poked our heads
In a cupboard in search of something salty
Or sweet, watching us through the blinds

As we walked to the door, as if we couldn't see
The shock of your red nails or how you hid
Your relief as you ran to greet us, pretending

You had been busy, not waiting all day in fear—
And what did you think would happen on the way,
What wolf or siren could interrupt our journey?

And why did you scream for me one night,
Pulling me too near, talking about a red hat
Your mother wore, your mother whose stroke

Left her mute, whom you nursed until the end?
Why did you sing about *shining a poor fence*
When you didn't want me to touch anything,

To leave your sight, so that the smell of freedom
Is the smell of paint on the wood frame
Of a windowpane I leaned against in winter.

Snow is falling in slow sumptuous flakes,
A squirrel is scurrying up a tree, collecting
The darts of the sun—it is gleeful,

It will claim for a time as its own
This short thick branch, dappled with moss
Underneath and a fine white powder on top.

I'm snug and warm in front of a double window,
Peering at trees in a field through leaded glass,
Thinking of you whom I seldom call to mind,

For you are the nebulous well of light
In your hazel eyes, the heavy arms that rolled
And cut the dough, the sullen queen

Who commanded my father, the tyrant who took
My mother and kept her a child, the brittle
Angel who floated through our house

After a stroke, pushing a walker and calling
For my mother as if she were yours.
You are the tired girl in a gossamer gown

Who lay in a hospital bed, following the image
On the ring on my finger—your eyes trailing
The motion of my hand the way an infant

In a cradle responds to a moving mobile
Or anything bright—the dove of Florence,
The tiny bird I dream will flee at night,

Leaving only an onyx sky, so that I wake
In my dream to the blindness of an eye
Without an iris, all pupil and no light.

O Nanny whose power petrified, whose pride
Flows in my blood so that I dread
My own strength, who knew I was in love

Before I knew, and knew this meant the end
Of love for you, all possession, all tenderness,
You had to close your heart

Before I could leave, and that is why
I have had to wait so long to call you back,
And am calling you now, asking you

To finish it for me:
Shine - a - Poor - Fen - ster—
It always breaks off there,

I cannot go further
Than *Fenster,* your song
Returns, why now, from where?

The words are almost gone,
What's left remains bewildering
And dear: tell me,

Is it a lullaby or a lament,
When did you learn to sing it,
Is anyone singing it to you,

What are you counting now, and who
Will shine the poor fence
Now that I know it wasn't ever there,

That *shina* is *pretty* and *poor* is *pair*
And all I have of you
Glimmers here—

A mound of snow melting into air,
Ice turning into lace,
Sheets of crystal, brilliant and bare,

Now that I see into
The two pretty windows
You are looking through,

O mountain of salt about to disappear.

PART THREE

Unsolicited Survey

Have you been there?

If so, can you describe the shape of the shadows?

When you entered, did anyone greet you?

Did the moss hug your foot or a jay screech in your ear?

Were you afraid you would not get back?

Did they ring a bell?

How many times, and what did it sound like?

Did a horse bow its head by the side of a road?

Did a single feather lie at the clearing?

Did a green wave cascade into a grove?

Did the flavor of light infect your sleep?

Did a toad leap from the dust onto a twig?

Did deer turn in terror as you passed?

Did a doe lick your hand and find you wanting?

Did you behold a flower that cannot fade?

Was the sky so empty that you fell upward?

Did the needles of a pine tickle your nose?

Did you sniff the ghost of the cedars of Lebanon?

Did you follow a petal blown to the edge of the sea?

Did you wake with a sheet twisted around your throat?

Did you call out?

Did you kneel at a blade of grass or the mound of an anthill?

Did you ask for a way in or a way out?

Did a bough sway imperceptibly?

Did you rest your hand on the shoulder of a god?

Did you open a piece of fruit and offer a portion of it to the sun?

How long did it take to finish, and were you satisfied?

Did a fly sip some water from a stone?

Did you touch the haze on a plum, its blue cloud?

Did you rub its skin until it lost its bloom?

Did the sun burn in a crow's eye?

Were the stars so clear another heaven appeared behind them?

Did you hear the wind consoling the leaves?

Did you look inside the cap of a mushroom, and part the curtain
    of disbelief?

Intervals in Early August

I.

I don't know how it is where you are now.
Mostly, I watch the trees move,
Though today they aren't doing much at all,
Except this instant when I wrote them down

And they began to sway the way they do
When a breeze out of nowhere stirs the air.
It seems the wind behaves erratically
As if to show us that we cannot say

What is sure without effacing it,
Or what is true without assuming light
Awakens beside a shadow of doubt.

Do you feel empty because the earth
Is full, and does a door slam shut
When a gust promises to change you?

to Goran in Hvar

II.

In the woods this morning a veil fell
Over everything, as if memory
Were in hiding and would not be back.
I almost panicked, then felt such relief

Untethered as that leaf upon the lake,
Not grieving or desiring anyone,
Content to look without a sense of loss
Until I saw another leaf nearby,

And focusing too long on the line
Between them created the illusion
Of a mirror holding nothing but a sky

Concealing nothing underneath, and all
At once I was dissolving into it
And in a moment the world could sink.

III.

In a second we were suspended
Like clouds in a bottomless chamber,
With no chance to alter shape or color,
Sentenced to float forever on a surface

That held the promise and the threat
Of changelessness, until a bubble
Newly forming on the lake
Glinted in the sun as it broke

Inaudibly into a ring of light
Whose radiating center disappeared.
A silver fish swam into sight,

Clearly going somewhere as well,
In deep enough waters off the shore
To live undisturbed by surfaces.

IV.

How would it sound if we could hear
The pop of that bubble,
Hovering there
Like a dragonfly at the exact interval?

What if we could enter
The fraction of time in which
A tadpole by the switch
Of a neurotransmitter

Turns from a darting creature
Into a frog who blinks on a lily-pad
Under the moon as a hand on a pad

Of paper scribbles notes on nature,
Trying to measure
All we are after?

On the Other Hand

The leaves of the ivy
Are heavy today.
Even we are too heavy,
Their shadows say:

Nothing moves us,
We cannot stray
Across a walkway.
But glory is still green.

Whoever leaned
Against a screen
Unlatches the door,

Whoever said
There, there, now
Doesn't anymore.

Soon

Something is always arriving or fading,
Drifting down a stream or falling
From branches into a pool of shade:

A cluster of hazelnuts lying in the grass
Of a summer garden soon, very soon
Graces a platter of olives and cheese

And green figs ripening since noon,
As we dine with the beautiful couple
At our table, drinking to the light

Between them a year before they part,
Confused and sad and sure, very sure
They cannot live together anymore.

The Blizzard

Now that the worst is over, they predict
Something messy and difficult, though not
Life-threatening. Clearly we needed

To stock up on water and candles, making
Tureens of soup and things that keep
When electricity fails and phone lines fall.

Igloos rise on air conditioners, gargoyles
Fly and icicles shatter. Frozen runways,
Lines in markets, and paralyzed avenues

Verify every fear. But there is warmth
In this sudden desire to sleep,
To surrender to our common condition

With joy, watching hours of news
Devoted to weather. People finally stop
To talk to each other—the neighbors

We didn't know were always here.
Today they are ready for business,
Armed with a new vocabulary,

Casting their saga in phrases as severe
As last night's snow: *damage assessment,*
Evacuation, emergency management.

The shift of the wind matters again,
And we are so simple, so happy to hear
The scrape of a shovel next door.

Company

When I rise from the rocker to cross
The room and sit in another chair

It is still rocking, the sound of a heart
Beating, a faint thump whose rhythm

Comforts before its unobtrusive source
Is recognized, drawing no attention

To itself to prove its presence
In the corner. People smoke because

A steady stream of breath the eye
Can see consoles them, confirming

They are not alone and can provide
For themselves. If I hear the cry

Of geese muffled by trees, and if
That sound repeated adds a star

To the flickering constellation
Of music, why can't love return

After it disappears, after the arrow
Leaving its bow loses itself

Among the rushes of the infinite?
Now those ragged cries recur more

Hurriedly, as if increase in persistence
And urgency means our arrival is near.

Futile Exercise

How do I put together
The way he gently held my finger,
Feeling for a splinter,

And the cruelty of later;
Or his thoughtlessness two years after,
When he invited me to dinner

In the final week of summer
And announced in less than an hour
That he was sorry

He had to be somewhere—
After noting how the grids of cities differ,
Then recalling his journey

To the prettiest place he'd ever been,
Where he took it easy
In a valley in Kentucky

Whose name alone was a pleasure
He wanted to share,
Though he changed the subject abruptly

The moment we smiled at each other;
How do I account for
His sudden interruption,

A conversation leading to terror
For no good reason,
And his courteous offer

To accompany me to the building
We lived in together,
Although we hadn't met in a year;

And how explain my rising
Sense of danger
As he said goodbye at the elevator

And I saw inside his opening door
Pieces of plaster
Covering the floor,

And then a week later
Saw the fracture
Running down his hallway mirror,

Repeating a riddle
No one could answer—
Why the scholar who was a dancer

Came to stand himself no longer;
Who can fit together
What made him show the super

A twisted chair his fist had beaten
Until it finally was broken,
And who can tell

Why days before
In the entrance hall
He stared at me, unblinking, feral,

And how connect the rampage of a mind
With a hand
So bent on order,

That cleaned the coffee pot completely
Or lowered the arm of a record player
Onto Mahler;

How do I put together
The hand that touched mine
And the cold revolver

Ending failure
When he pulled the trigger
With the finger that found

The splinter
He was after
Before

Georgic

in memory of Edward Thomas

If walking down a country lane
You stop to look at gathering clouds
And feel your life a prison-house,
Then think of sky

Open as pastures brushed by dew,
Mountains brightening
After thunder passes through,
A feather wavering in the light;

Or think of one
Who made a midnight requiem
From the rainfall

Of falling men,
As he lay unsleeping in mud
Warmer than some.

In a Haystack

Nothing, no one now, will ever find me,
Even in a thousand years, climbing

Everest or Aetna, fathoming leaves
Doe-brown, dry as a freckled shell

Left on a moon-lit beach, needing
Every drop it cannot drink.

Integer of light in a sheaf of light,
Not here, not far, sharp as a star:

And how will anyone know I ever was?
How will the wind piercing the rafters

Answer my stillness, undo the pattern
Yesterday left behind when Mother

Set down her basket, forgetting
To tuck me in for the night.

At first I revelled in my release:
Cut loose, no fetters

Kept me close to a human hand.
If only someone would light a match

To set me free, razing this hill
Until nothing else remains—

So the wind can reach me again
And someone carefully lift me,

Warm me and carry me home
Where I can lie, knowing someone

Will slip a thread through my eye,
Pulling me through luminous waves,

Using me for something she needs
Before putting me down.

The Lector

Row after row of benches, like pews,
Though a scent not of incense
But tobacco, leaves picked long ago,

Resting on tables where everyone
Is leaning over his lot, ready to work
Again, waiting for the words to begin.

Sometimes they want a new one,
A story never read to them before
Or verses they haven't heard recited

In the voice of that reader: sometimes
It's Cervantes, *El Cid,* or Homer,
Then they go back to *Monte Cristo.*

Line upon line fills them as they
Finish one, setting a leaf aside
To bind another, hearing centuries

Compress into a phrase as feeling
Unfurls its banner in the shade.
Somewhere across a bay or across

The sea, someone is leaning back
To savor a cigar rolled to a stanza
Of Góngora or Quevedo, guided

By a hero or a fool, or a love
Imprisoned and on fire, fed
By the arms of a windmill

Whose power daily proves
How little is needed to kindle
A dream, how much

To make a life bearable—a leaf
Slowly burning, a single aroma
As rich as illusion,

A form that will be
Undone by a breath,
Changing into nothing in his hand.

Confession of an Alchemist

All my intentions failed.
When I wanted to enter the mountain
A dragon roared, when I wanted to enter the sky
A giant cloud drove me back to earth.
The river brought me nowhere, even a stream
Broke my will, and the pebbles in a brook
Chanted lies to my believing ears.

No one comforted me, no one
Looked over my shoulder or carried me home.
Once you glinted like ice burning in sunlight,
Sometimes you touched my fingers in the rain
Or appeared at a roadside at night as a spotted doe.
But I did not stroke you, did not feed you
Bread from my mouth or hand.

The willows grew too heavy,
Uprooting my heart, like a hundred maidens
Brushing their hair in the dark
Without knowing someone with hair as thick as theirs
Waited near them in moonlight, standing alone.
When you turned and saw me, I turned and saw
Both of us watching.

At the sound of your voice I fled
From you without moving, when you opened your eyes
I was afraid you would see what you had done.
But you saw nothing, you smiled without shame.
How could I take the salt from your hand
When the scent of your skin drew me into a wood
Whose leaves fall without end.

Nothing was spoken, everything fulfilled,
Everything shattered, as if it were foretold.
I did not want to become a laurel tree,
You did not want to be caught or torn apart,
And nothing can close the space between us now.
Only our hands are the same, but all we do
With them is draw lead from gold.

Meditation on A and The

Last night the world reduced itself to *a* and *the*
And for a number of numberless hours

Everyone spoke in a language combining
The two, like the binary code of zero

And one, or the never-ending tango
Of two pairs of nucleotides,

The series of couplets
Determining who we are,

So that every hesitation
Was not a stutter but a meaning,

Though every sentence sounded
Like a stutter.

But what is an article, anyway,
And how definite can a definite article be

When it renders something more abstract,
Not less, just by saying *the*

Instead of *thee;*
And what about the definiteness of *a,*

That is, for instance, of a pear,
Which means a thing apart from anything else:

The pear on the table is not just a pear
But *the* pear, but the pear soon becomes

More than a pear, and so less,
Because it enters the realm of pearness,

A rather peerless place to be.
Is the quality of pear

Like the quality of mercy,
And does anyone have mercy on *the* and *a,*

Such as the mercy of those who are merciful
And those who are not, i.e., the merciless?

Notice how the ones who have mercy
Do not easily attach themselves to an article,

How the table on which you work
Was a table for a while, before it became

The table where you work: you wanted a table,
You got a table, now it is

The table you know so well, nothing like
A table belonging to anyone else.

And if you met a friend who was the friend
Of another, you might say to him or to her,

Aren't you a friend of so and so,
An old friend, a new friend,

A real friend, even a *true* friend—
But *the* true friend, that would be too much,

As if there were only one, and sooner or later
Not the only one but the word standing

For all of the ones who are true,
A true friend becoming one of the true.

How large, how magnanimous a noun grows
Without one: mountains are definitely bigger

Than *the* mountains, more visible, too,
Which leads to the way an article behaves

In the presence of the plural, how *the* may go
Before one or many, whereas the indefinite

Dwells with the singular exclusively,
In which case an article often slips in

Even when an adjective precedes:
Blue dresses blow in the breeze

Very easily, but one blue dress
Depends on *one* to elude an *a* or a *the*.

Soon there will be snow, it
Will snow, the *it* will be the snow

That will fall, the flakes will sink
To earth, the earth we know, an earth

Like no other, and then the *the* will be
An *a* again, the *a* that follows *the* the way

You want to hear a story, the one
You heard before, the way the gods

Became a god who made,
It is said, a world, an evening

And a morning on the first day,
Before the verb became

A noun, before the god
Became a god who called the day

A day, and what a day it was,
What a day, what a day.

About the Author

Phillis Levin is the author of *Temples and Fields* (University of Georgia Press, 1988), winner of the Poetry Society of America's Norma Farber First Book Award, and *The Afterimage* (Copper Beech Press, 1995). Her poems have appeared in *The New Bread Loaf Anthology of Contemporary American Poetry, The Best American Poetry 1998, The New Yorker, Paris Review, Poetry, Partisan Review, The New Criterion, Agni, The Atlantic, Grand Street, The Nation, PN Review, Kenyon Review, The New Republic, TriQuarterly, Ploughshares,* and *The Best American Poetry 1989.* Translations of her poems have been published in Peru, Argentina, Slovenia, Poland, Hungary, Russia, and Israel. Levin has been a resident fellow at The MacDowell Colony and Yaddo, and was a Bogliasco Fellow at the Liguria Study Center for the Arts and Humanities in Italy. She has received, among other honors, an Ingram Merrill Grant, a Fulbright fellowship to Slovenia, and the Amy Lowell Poetry Travelling Scholarship. She is also the editor of an anthology, *The Penguin Book of the Sonnet.*

Born in Paterson, New Jersey, and educated at Sarah Lawrence College and The Johns Hopkins University, Phillis Levin has taught at the University of Maryland, College Park, and the Unterberg Poetry Center of the 92nd Street Y. She is now professor of English and Poet-in-Residence at Hofstra University, and lives in New York City.

Ted Berrigan	*Selected Poems*
Ted Berrigan	*The Sonnets*
Philip Booth	*Lifelines*
Philip Booth	*Pairs*
Jim Carroll	*Fear of Dreaming*
Jim Carroll	*Void of Course*
Nicholas Christopher	*5 & Other Poems*
Diane di Prima	*Loba*
Stuart Dischell	*Evenings & Avenues*
Stephen Dobyns	*Common Carnage*
Stephen Dobyns	*Pallbearers Envying the One Who Rides*
Paul Durcan	*A Snail in My Prime*
Amy Gerstler	*Crown of Weeds*
Amy Gerstler	*Medicine*
Amy Gerstler	*Nerve Storm*
Debora Greger	*Desert Fathers, Uranium Daughters*
Robert Hunter	*Glass Lunch*
Robert Hunter	*Sentinel*
Barbara Jordan	*Trace Elements*
Jack Kerouac	*Book of Blues*
Ann Lauterbach	*And For Example*
Ann Lauterbach	*If in Time*
Ann Lauterbach	*On a Stair*
Phillis Levin	*Mercury*
William Logan	*Night Battle*
William Logan	*Vain Empires*
Derek Mahon	*Selected Poems*
Michael McClure	*Huge Dreams: San Francisco and Beat Poems*
Michael McClure	*Three Poems*
Carol Muske	*An Octave Above Thunder*
Alice Notley	*The Descent of Alette*

Alice Notley	*Mysteries of Small Houses*
Lawrence Raab	*The Probable World*
Anne Waldman	*Kill or Cure*
Anne Waldman	*Marriage: A Sentence*
Rachel Wetzsteon	*Home and Away*
Philip Whalen	*Overtime: Selected Poems*
Robert Wrigley	*In the Bank of Beautiful Sins*
Robert Wrigley	*Reign of Snakes*